# THE STORY OF BARACK OBAMA

## A Biography Book for New Readers

Written by
**TONYA LESLIE, PhD**

Illustrated by
**LORIS LORA**

ROCKRIDGE PRESS

**To children everywhere.**
**You are the hope of the future.**



Series Designer: Angela Navarra

Interior and Cover Designer: Jane Archer

Art Producer: Hannah Dickerson

Editor: Kristen Depken

Production Editor: Nora Milman

Author Photo courtesy of Christina Morassi

Illustrator Photo courtesy of Sam Kimbrell

Illustrations © Loris Lora, 2020. Maps courtesy of Creative Market. Photographs: Shutterstock/s_bukley, p. 50; Alamy Stock Photo/White House Photo, p. 52; Shutterstock/Evan El-Amin, p. 53.

ISBN: Print 978-1-64739-105-8 | eBook 978-1-64739-106-5

R02

Printed in China

# CONTENTS

## CHAPTER 1

# A PRESIDENT IS BORN

# Meet Barack

There was never anything ordinary about Barack Hussein Obama. When he became the 44th **president** of the United States, people took note. He was one of the youngest presidents. He was also the first black president! His life was an extraordinary journey that spanned the globe, eventually leading him to the White House.

Barack was born in Honolulu, Hawaii, in 1961. Hawaii had recently become the 50th state in the United States. It is the only state made up of islands! Barack grew up in this tropical paradise surrounded by the Pacific Ocean. He is probably the only president to grow up surfing and eating sushi.

Life for the 44th president was unique. He lived in many different cities in the United States, including New York, Chicago, and Los Angeles. He also lived in the country of Indonesia and visited Kenya, a country in Africa. Barack learned about the different ways that people lived. He saw people who were suffering and decided that he wanted to spend his life helping others. He worked hard to become a **lawyer**, then a **senator**, and then the president of the United States, all so that he could change people's lives for the better. And he did!

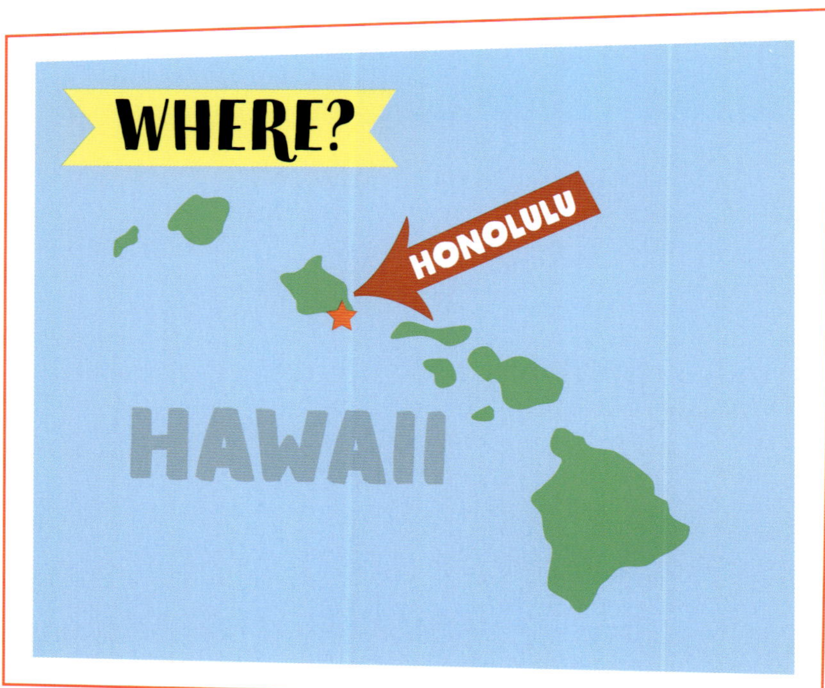

## Barack's America

Barack was born in Honolulu, the capital city of Hawaii, on August 4, 1961. Hawaii is thousands of miles from the rest of the United States, in the middle of the Pacific Ocean. Barack's parents were not born in Hawaii. His mother, Ann, was a white woman born in Kansas. She had moved to Honolulu with her family. Barack's father was named Barack, too. He was a black man who was born in Kenya. He had moved to Honolulu to study.

## JUMP IN THE THINK TANK

Barack Obama grew up on the unique islands of Hawaii. What's unique about where you live? What do you like best about it?

When Ann and Barack met, the marriage of a black man and a white woman was **controversial**. There were laws in the United States in the 1960s that kept black and white people apart. In some states, it was against the law for black and white people to sit at the same lunch counter, sit next to each other on the bus, or even drink from the same water fountain.

Because of these laws, Barack's family would not have been safe in some parts of

## MYTH & FACT

**MYTH:** Black people and white people have always been able to get married.

**FACT:** In some states, it was illegal for black people and white people to get married until 1967.

the United States, but they were safe in Hawaii. The laws keeping people apart didn't exist there. Hawaii's **population** was made up of many different people with many different skin colors. Barack's family was different, but other families in Hawaii were different, too.

Barack grew up meeting a lot of people. Some looked like him, and some looked different. But it didn't matter. In Hawaii, there were no laws that could limit where he could go and how he could live. Barack grew up feeling like he was free to dream and be whatever he wanted.

## WHEN?

**1959** — Hawaii becomes the 50th state.

**1960** — John F. Kennedy is elected 35th President of the United States.

**1961** — Barack Obama is born.

# CHAPTER 2

# THE EARLY YEARS

# Growing Up in Paradise

When Barack was very young, his mother and father got a **divorce**. His father moved back to his home country, Kenya. Barack stayed in Hawaii with his mother and his grandparents, who he called Gramps and Toot. They called him Barry.

Barry loved Hawaii. He spent a lot of time with Gramps and Toot while his mother studied. She was a student at the University of Hawaii. She enjoyed learning about different **cultures** and shared what she learned with Barry. While she was studying, Barry spent a lot of time outdoors. He loved to swim and surf. He also loved food and would eat raw fish called **sashimi**.

Hawaii is a tropical place. There are beaches, mountains, and even volcanoes. Astronauts would train in Hawaii because the land there was similar to the land on Mars. Once, Barry sat

on Gramps's shoulders and waved an American flag at astronauts returning from the moon.

Life in Hawaii felt very full. But something was missing. Barry's dad had moved back to Kenya when Barry was young. Barry didn't remember a lot about him, but he knew they shared the same name. He also knew that his dad looked different than his mom and grandparents. His dad was black, and the rest of his family was white. That meant Barry looked different than his mom and grandparents, too. He knew that the color of his skin meant something to a lot of people, but he didn't understand why. He wished his father was around to help him understand that part of himself.

When Barry was three, his mom met a new friend named Lolo at school. He was kind to Barry. Barry was happy when his mother told him she was going to marry Lolo, and that Lolo would be his stepfather.

## The Obama Family

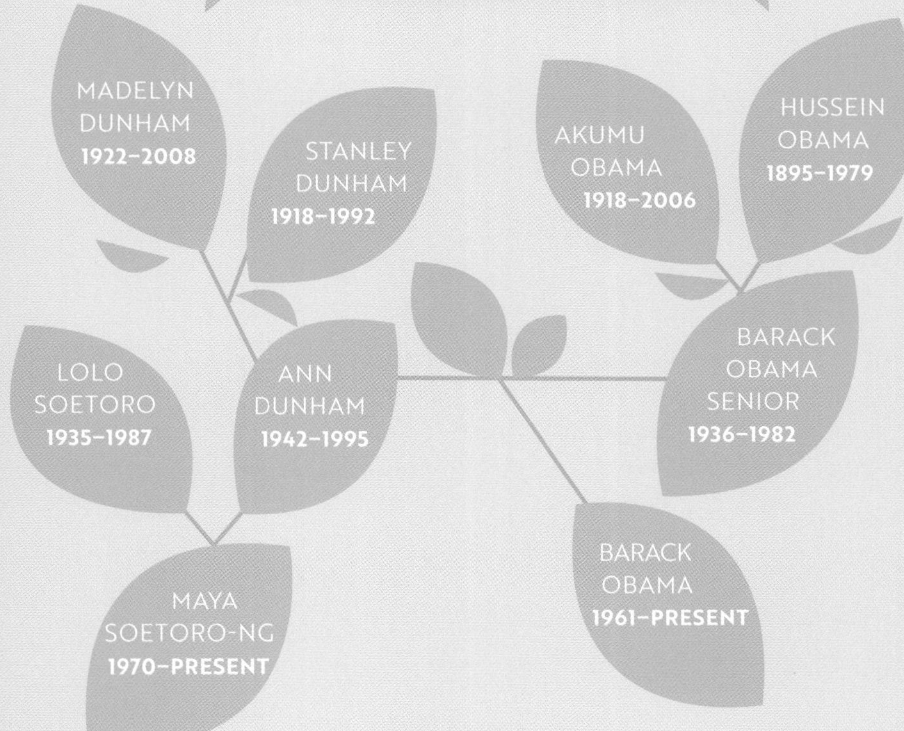

## Moving to Indonesia

Lolo was from a country called Indonesia. After he and Barry's mom got married, Lolo had to return to Indonesia. It was a group of islands, like Hawaii, and very far away. In 1967, Barry's mom decided that she and Barry would live in Indonesia with Lolo. They would have to take a long plane ride to get there.

It was hard for Barry to leave everyone he loved, especially Gramps and Toot, but the

journey to Indonesia felt like an adventure. Barry's mom wanted to teach Barry about new countries and new cultures, so they visited other places along the way.

When they finally got to Indonesia, they landed in a city called Jakarta. Lolo was very happy to see them. He even gave Barry a pet ape named Tata! Barry liked to explore Jakarta

## JUMP IN THE THINK TANK

Barry moved to a new country when he was very young. What do you think he learned from living in Indonesia? Do you think you would like to live in another country?

with Lolo. They ate different types of food, like snake meat and roasted grasshoppers! Barry loved these adventures, but his mom wanted him to keep up with his studies.

**MYTH & FACT**

| MYTH | FACT |
| --- | --- |
| Barack isn't a **citizen** of the United States because he lived in Indonesia. | Barack was born in Hawaii. He is an American citizen. |

At a school near his house, Barry was learning about Indonesia and its culture. His mother wanted him to learn about American history, too, so she began to teach him. They learned about **civil rights** and how black people in the United States were fighting to do things like vote and get an education. Then Barry's mom had another baby. Barry loved his little sister Maya. But Barry's mom wasn't able to spend as much time teaching him anymore. She worried that he wasn't getting the education he needed. She sent him back to Hawaii so he could live with Gramps and Toot and go to school.

## WHEN?

| 1967 | 1970 | 1971 |
| --- | --- | --- |
| Barry and his mother move to Indonesia. | Barry's sister Maya is born. | Barry moves back to Hawaii. |

# CHAPTER 3

# GETTING AN EDUCATION

## A Special Visitor

Barry returned to Hawaii in 1971 to live with Gramps and Toot. He started attending a new school and became very interested in his studies. Then one day Gramps and Toot told Barry that his dad was coming to visit for a month.

Barry missed his father. He had always wanted to get to know his dad better. But he hadn't seen him in eight years. Barry worried. Would they get along? Would his father be proud of him?

When Barry's dad arrived, there were some challenges. Barry didn't like it when his father tried to tell him what to do. But there were good times, too. Barry and his dad took long walks. His dad talked about his life in Hawaii and showed Barry all the places that were special to him.

One day, Barry's dad came to his school to speak. At first, Barry was nervous. But Barry's classmates loved hearing his father talk about life in Kenya. He told them about the wild animals that lived there and how his country struggled to be free. Barry was proud of his father's stories. He began to see that they were his stories, too.

## Study Period

After his father left, Barry stayed busy with school. He loved to read, but he sometimes struggled with his schoolwork. He learned how to drive and got a job after school. But his favorite thing was basketball. He played on his high school team, and he was good. Sometimes when Barry went to games at

### JUMP IN THE THINK TANK

Barry was nervous about his father's visit. Why do you think he felt nervous? Have you ever felt nervous to see someone?

other schools, people said hurtful things to him because of the color of his skin. Barry wanted to understand why skin color mattered so much. He began to study the lives of people who had skin like his. He read books by black writers like James Baldwin and Malcolm X. The more he learned about the types of **injustice** people faced because of their skin color, the more he wanted to fight against it.

> "America is a place where you can write your own destiny."

Black people everywhere were fighting against this injustice, too. The **Civil Rights Movement** helped change laws in America to give people of all skin colors **equal rights**, but it took a long time for people's hearts to change. Black people were still facing **discrimination**.

Barry wanted to understand how people changed things in history. He believed he could change things, too.

## WHEN?

Barry's father comes to visit from Kenya.

**1971**

Barry graduates high school in Hawaii.

**1979**

# CHAPTER 4
# BECOMING BARACK

## Off to College

In 1979, Barack left Hawaii to go to Occidental College in Los Angeles, California. He still wanted to help people and make a change in the world, so he studied **political science** and **international affairs**. He also made one big change. He decided to stop going by his childhood nickname. He no longer felt like Barry the boy. Now he felt like Barack the man. As Barack, he wanted to make a difference in the world.

After two years, Barack transferred to Columbia University in New York City. He continued to study **politics**. New York City was exciting but a little lonely. Barack spent a lot of his time studying alone. When his mother came to visit, she worried that he was becoming too serious. Barack thought it was important to stay focused on trying to help others.

Then, Barack received a letter from his father. He invited Barack to come visit him in Kenya.

Barack was excited. He had a whole family in Kenya that he wanted to meet. He would learn more about his father and himself. But then, a terrible thing happened. Barack's father died in a car accident.

Barack's heart was heavy. He studied more. He graduated from Columbia and got a job as a researcher and writer. But what he wanted to do most was help people in the **community**. He felt better when he helped others. Barack

> We are the change that we seek.

decided he wanted to be a **community organizer**. He moved to Chicago, Illinois, and did just that.

As a community organizer, Barack brought people together to solve problems in their neighborhoods. Barack worked with churches to do things like create after-school programs for children. He created training programs to help

people find jobs and support their families. But it didn't feel like enough. Barack saw that laws had to change in order for people to get the things they needed. He decided to go to law school to help people fight for the **justice** they deserved.

## Visiting Kenya

Barack thought about his father and his family in Kenya a lot. When he had some time before starting law school, he finally took a trip to Kenya. Barack felt at home right away. A woman at the airport recognized his name and knew his father. Barack met his aunts, uncles, and many cousins. He met a woman he called Granny, but learned she wasn't his real grandmother. That was the interesting thing about Kenya. Barack found that people were very strongly connected, even when they were not related by blood.

## JUMP IN THE THINK TANK

Barack met a lot of family he didn't know in Kenya. It made him think about what makes a family. Is it the people you are born to or the people you love?

Barack spent weeks in Kenya. Each day, he learned new things about his father. He learned that his father had been a brilliant student. He met his father's other children, who were his half brothers and sisters.

Barack learned a lot about the country of Kenya. He went on **safari** and saw lions, elephants, giraffes, and many other animals. It reminded him of the stories his father had told his classmates long ago. It was a special time. When it was time to leave, Barack felt changed. He had found a new place to call home.

## WHEN?

**1979** — Barack starts college in Los Angeles.

**1981** — Barack transfers to Columbia University in New York City.

**1982** — Barack's father dies in a car accident.

**1983** — Barack graduates from Columbia University.

**1985** — Barack moves to Chicago.

**1987** — Barack visits Kenya.

# CHAPTER 5

# A NEW CAREER

## Barack the Lawyer

When Barack returned from Kenya, he planned to go to law school at Harvard University in Cambridge, Massachusetts. Harvard is one of the best law schools in the United States, and Barack's father had studied there. Barack felt that going to Harvard would give him the education he needed to make a difference not just for his community in the United States, but also for his family in Kenya.

Barack knew exactly what he wanted to do. He wanted to be a civil rights lawyer and fight for justice. Barack studied hard. In 1990, he became president of the *Harvard Law Review*, an important **journal** run by students. He was the first African American to be chosen for that role.

Barack's time at Harvard was busy. During summers he worked at a law firm in Chicago.

He was introduced to a **mentor** named Michelle Robinson. She had also gone to Harvard and would help Barack learn more about the law firm. Barack and Michelle soon fell in love. When Barack graduated from Harvard in 1991, he returned to Chicago to be closer to Michelle. He took a job as a civil rights lawyer and worked to help people fight for their rights.

## JUMP IN THE THINK TANK

Many presidents have been lawyers. How might being a lawyer help someone prepare to be president?

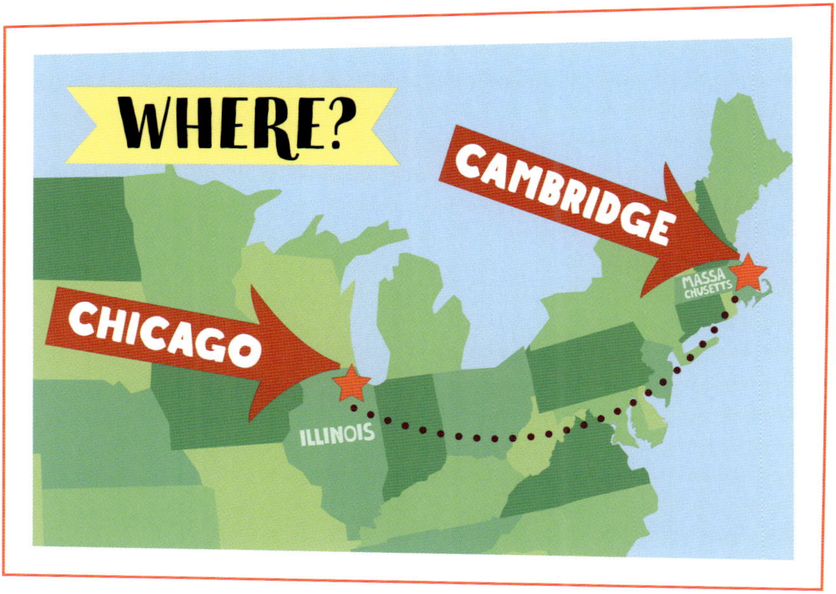

## ★ Senator Obama ★

Barack and Michelle got married in 1992. They both shared an interest in helping people. Michelle worked at an organization that helped young people get involved in their communities. Barack decided he could help people by being a part of the government. He ran for the position of senator in the state of Illinois. A state senator works to create laws. Many people voted for Barack and he won! Barack helped pass laws that helped people get better jobs, find **affordable** childcare, and make their neighborhoods safer.

Even though Chicago was now home for Barack, he went back to Hawaii as much as he could. His mother lived there and she was sick. He tried to see her as often as he could, but it was hard with all his responsibilities in Chicago. Plus, Barack was writing a book about his life.

His mother died in 1995, just a few months after his book was published.

Barack worked even harder after his mother died. When he ran for **reelection** as state senator, he easily won. He served three **terms**. His book was published and won awards. Now even people outside of Chicago knew who Barack was.

Meanwhile, Barack and Michelle were starting a family. In 1998, their daughter Malia Ann was born. Three years later, they welcomed another baby girl. They named her Natasha but called her by her nickname, Sasha. Barack's family was growing, his career was growing, and everyone wondered what he would do next.

> Being a father is sometimes my hardest but always my most rewarding job.

## WHEN?

| | |
|---|---|
| 1991 | Barack graduates from Harvard. |
| 1992 | Barack and Michelle get married. |
| 1995 | Barack's mother dies. |
| 1998 | Malia is born. |
| 2001 | Sasha is born. |

# CHAPTER 6
# WORKING FOR CHANGE

## A New Role

Barack enjoyed working as a state senator for the people in Illinois, but he thought that he could make a greater difference. He wanted to support his **political party** by running for a different position. In the United States there are two major political groups: the Republican Party and the Democratic Party. In 2004, Barack wrote and delivered a big **speech** at the Democratic National Convention, the event where the Democratic Party announces their **candidate** for president.

Barack got a lot of attention for his speech. He spoke about his family's story and how it inspired him to have hope for the future. His words excited people. When he ran for the role of United States senator from Illinois in 2004, he easily won.

In this new role, Barack worked to help people across the country. He helped create a law that stopped soldiers from being treated unfairly. He served on a committee to help protect the environment. He liked his work, but there was one downside. He missed his family.

Being a United States senator meant spending more time in Washington, DC. Michelle didn't want to move the family, so they decided that she and the children would stay in Chicago. Barack would travel back and forth to DC. As a United States senator, Barack worked to create and vote

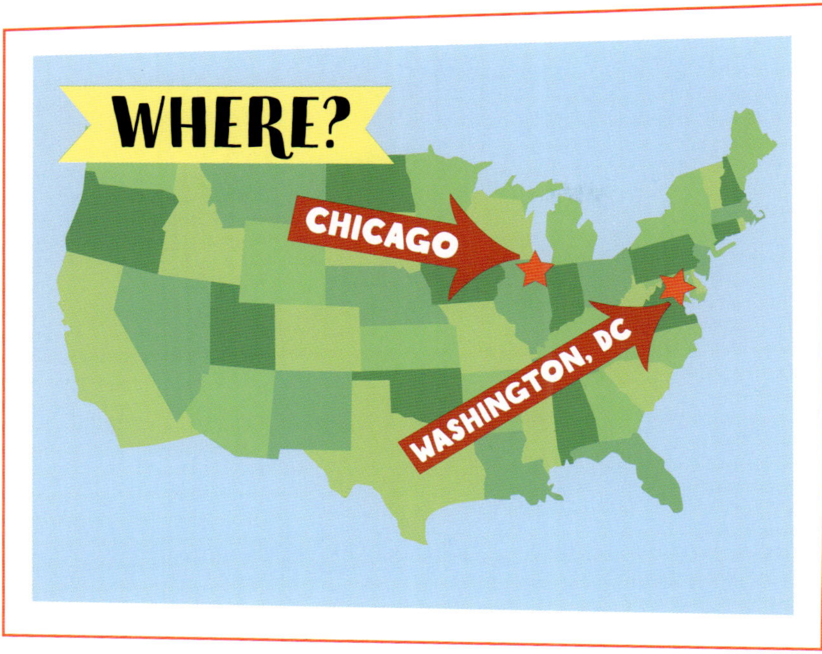


for laws that would help a lot of people. It was good work, but he still wanted to do more. He began to think about running for president.

## Running for President

Barack thought that if he were president, he would be able to make real change happen for people throughout the United States. But he and Michelle knew that running for president would change their lives, too.

## MYTH & FACT

**MYTH:** There's only one type of senator.

**FACT:** There are two: a state senator and a US senator. Barack was both!

They were worried about how it would affect their family if Barack became president. They would have to leave Chicago, where they had family and friends. Malia and Sasha would have to grow up in the White House. Barack and Michelle talked it over with their family. Then they made a decision. Barack would run for president in 2008 against another senator named John McCain. Barack made a promise to his daughters: If he became president, they could finally get a dog!

To become president, Barack would have to run a political **campaign**. During a campaign, a person tries to become well-known and share their ideas so that people will vote for them and put them in **office**. A lot of people already knew Barack

because of his book and his work as a senator, but the campaign helped even more people learn about him. Images of Barack were everywhere. Thousands of people came out to hear him speak.

On the campaign trail, Barack once again spoke about hope. He spoke about the need for strong leaders who wanted to work for change. People

## JUMP IN THE THINK TANK

Hope was a big theme in Barack's campaign. Why do you think Barack made people feel hopeful?

grew more and more excited about Barack's campaign. He was young and he was different. People felt like it was time for a change.

November 4, 2008, was election day. Once the votes were counted it became clear: Barack had won! He would be the 44th president of the United States—and the first African American president. It was a historic day.

## WHEN?

| Barack speaks at the Democratic National Convention. | Barack becomes a US senator. | Barack starts his presidential campaign. | Barack wins the election to become president! |
|---|---|---|---|
| **2004** | **2004** | **2007** | **2008** |

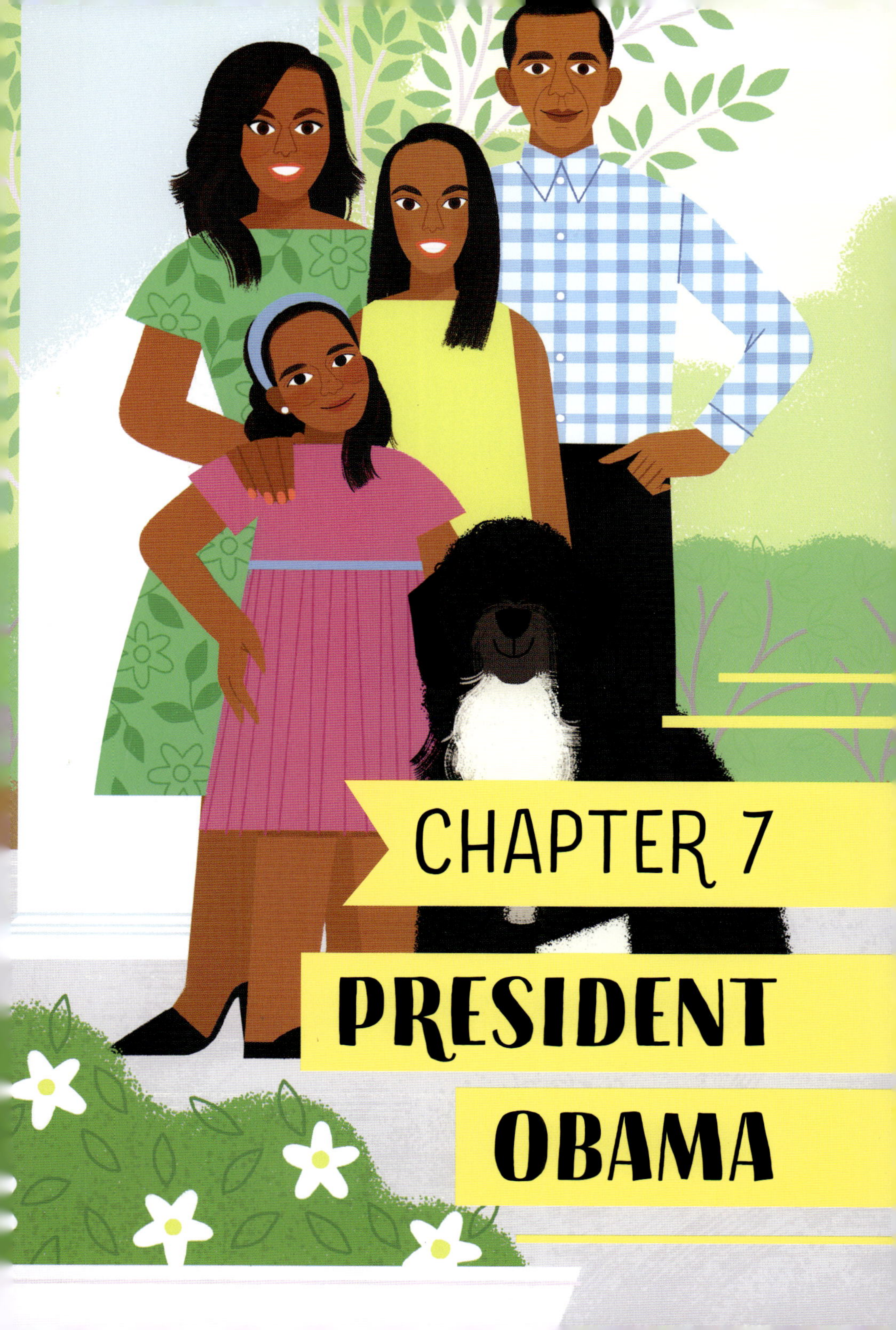

# CHAPTER 7
# PRESIDENT OBAMA

# Moving into the White House

Barack's job as president started on January 20, 2009. That's the day that he, Michelle, and the girls moved into the White House, just like every other president has since 1800.

The White House is an odd place to call home. It's old. It was built over 200 years ago. It's busy. Thousands of people visit every day. It's also huge. It has 132 rooms!

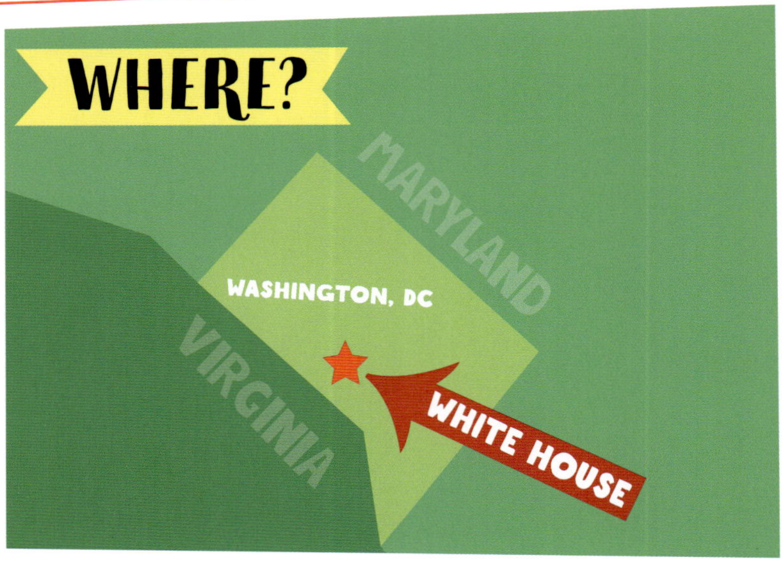

## MYTH & FACT

**MYTH:** Barack wasn't able to use **social media** as president.

**FACT:** Barack is considered the first social media president. He was the first president to send a tweet from the Oval Office.

Barack and Michelle wanted to make the White House feel like home, so they brought their own furniture with them. They also tried to keep their lives as normal as possible. Even though the White House has a cleaning staff, Malia and Sasha still had to do chores like making their beds. They had sleepovers and pizza parties just like other kids their age.

Meanwhile, Barack was working hard as president. One of the first things he did was try to make the **economy** grow. He helped people get jobs and cut **taxes** to help people save money. He made changes that would help people win the right to marry anyone they wanted. He also ended a war in the country of Iraq that had been going on for a long time.

In 2010, Barack signed a law called the Affordable Care Act. This law would help people be able to go to doctors and hospitals when they were sick. The program would cost the government a lot of money. Some people didn't want the law to pass. But it did, and a lot of people got the care they needed.

Barack did a lot in his first four years in office, including keeping his promise to Sasha and Malia. The girls finally got a puppy! They named him Bo.

## A Second Term

A president can only serve for four years at a time. Then they must run for reelection to be the president for another term, or four more years. A person can only be president for eight years total. In 2012, it was time for Barack to run again.

He ran against a former Massachusetts governor named Mitt Romney. It was a tough election. The country was growing divided. Some people liked what Barack was doing, but some people did not. Still, Barack won.

He knew it would be his final four years as president, so he tried to push for even bigger changes. He fought for new laws to help the environment. He changed policies to protect young people in America who came from other countries.

## JUMP IN THE THINK TANK

Why do you think Barack wanted to run for a second term as president? Do you think presidents should be allowed to stay in office for longer than two terms?

Barack's last day in office was January 20, 2017. The first thing he wanted to do after being president for eight years was take a long vacation with his family! He took them to Indonesia, where he used to live. Life after the White House seemed slower. Barack felt he finally had time to think about all the things that had happened in those eight years.

After their vacation, Barack and Michelle stayed in Washington, DC, so that Sasha could finish high school there. Malia was going to Harvard University—just like her dad. Barack decided that he didn't want to keep working in politics. Instead he wanted to make change in other ways. He and Michelle started an organization in Chicago to help young people get education

and jobs. They began writing books and even making films. They hope their work will educate and inspire people.

Barack Obama's story will always remind people that no matter where we come from, we can find hope in our own stories, work toward change, and achieve big things.

# WHEN?

Barack is sworn in as president.

**2009**

The Affordable Care Act becomes law.

**2010**

The Iraq War ends.

**2011**

Barack is elected for a second term.

**2012**

Barack's last day as president.

**2017**

# CHAPTER 8

# SO...WHO IS BARACK OBAMA?

# Challenge Accepted!

Now that you have learned all about Barack Obama, let's test your new knowledge in a little who, what, when, where, why, and how quiz. Feel free to look back in the text to find the answers if you need to, but try to remember first!

**1 Where was Barack born?**

→ A Jakarta, Indonesia
→ B Kenya, Africa
→ C Honolulu, Hawaii
→ D Washington, DC

**2 What was Barack's nickname?**

→ A Barry
→ B Rocky
→ C Obama
→ D Junior

**3** **Who is Barack's wife?**

→ A Sasha
→ B Malia
→ C Michelle
→ D Mary

**4** **Which school did Barack NOT go to?**

→ A Columbia University
→ B Occidental College
→ C Harvard University
→ D New York University

**5** **Which job did Barack have before becoming president?**

→ A Community organizer
→ B Civil rights lawyer
→ C Senator
→ D All of the above

**6** **What year was Barack elected president?**

- A 1961
- B 2008
- C 2017
- D 2000

**7** **How many terms did Barack serve as president?**

- A One
- B Two
- C Three
- D Four

**8** **What type of pet did the first family get?**

- A A cat
- B A dog
- C A turtle
- D A rabbit

**9** **What were some ways Barack tried to make a better world?**

→ A He helped people find jobs.

→ B He tried to help the environment.

→ C He helped people get health care.

→ D All of the above

**10** **Where did Malia go to school?**

→ A Columbia University

→ B Occidental College

→ C Harvard University

→ D New York University

**Answers:** 1. C; 2. A; 3. C; 4. D; 5. D; 6. B; 7. B; 8. B; 9. D; 10. C

## Our World

Like all presidents, Barack Obama will be remembered by history. Let's look at how the work of the 44th president will live on!

→ Barack made history. He became the first African American president. Many Americans felt hopeful that his election showed that the country was changing and that skin color didn't matter.

→ Barack helped people stay healthy. He helped make sure Americans had health care they could afford by passing the Affordable Care Act.

→ Barack helped the environment by creating laws to limit pollution and protect the climate.

# JUMP IN THE THINK TANK FOR MORE!

Now let's think a little more about what Barack Obama did and how he made a difference as the 44th president of the United States.

→ Barack broke a lot of barriers in his life. He was the first black editor of the *Harvard Law Review*. He was the first black president. What does it mean to be the first? What might be some benefits and challenges of being the first to do something?

→ Barack's passion was helping people. How do you think his early work helping people prepared him to be president?

→ Barack's daughters grew up in the White House. What might be some benefits of growing up in the White House? What might be some challenges?

# Glossary

**affordable:** Not too expensive

**campaign:** The activities that help a person reach a goal

**candidate:** A person who wants to be elected to a role in government

**citizen:** A person who legally belongs to a country or place

**civil rights:** Basic rights that every person has under the laws of the government

**Civil Rights Movement:** A time of struggle during the 1950s and 1960s when black people in America fought for equal rights

**community:** A group of people living or working together

**community organizer:** A person who works to help the members of a community

**controversial:** Relating to or causing disagreement or argument

**cultures:** The ways of life for a group of people, including their food, language, clothing, tools, music, art, beliefs, and religion

**discrimination:** The unfair treatment of a person or group of people

**divorce:** The legal ending of a marriage between two people

**economy:** The system of how money is made and used

**equal rights:** The ability of all people to have the same treatment, opportunities, responsibilities, and freedoms

**injustice:** An act or behavior that's not right, fair, or equal

**international affairs:** Relationships between different countries and their governments

**journal:** A magazine about a particular professional subject

**justice:** Fairness

**lawyer:** A person who is trained in understanding laws

**mentor:** Someone who teaches or helps another person

**office:** A role or position in government

**political party:** A group of people who share similar ideas and goals about government

**political science:** The study of government

**politics:** Activities related to the government of a city, state, country, or nation

**population:** The people who live in a certain place

**president:** The elected leader of a country or organization

**reelection:** The act of being elected again for a role that is already held

**safari:** A trip to see animals living in the wild

**sashimi:** Thinly sliced raw fish

**senator:** A person who is elected to work in the government

**social media:** Electronic communications that allow people to connect with one another

**speech:** A formal talk given to an audience

**taxes:** Money the government collects from citizens to help pay for things

**term:** The amount of time that a person is allowed to hold an elected position in government

# Bibliography

The American Presidency Project. "Welcome to The American Presidency Project." 2020. Presidency.UCSB.edu.

Bogost, Ian. "Obama Was Too Good at Social Media." *The Atlantic.* January 6, 2017. TheAtlantic.com/technology/archive/2017/01/did-america-need-a-social-media-president/512405.

*Columbia News.* "President Barack Obama, Columbia Graduate, Is Inaugurated for Second Term." January 20, 2013. News.Columbia.edu/news/president-barack-obama-columbia-graduate-inaugurated-second-term.

*Harvard Law Today.* "Obama first made history at HLS." November 1, 2008. Today.Law.Harvard.edu/obama-first-made-history-at-hls.

Maraniss, David. "Barack Obama: the college years." *The Guardian.* May 25, 2012. TheGuardian.com/world/2012/may/25/barack-obama-the-college-years.

Obama, Barack. *Dreams from My Father: A Story of Race and Inheritance.* Edinburgh: Canongate Books, 2007.

Obama, Barack. *The Audacity of Hope: Thoughts on Reclaiming the American Dream.* Edinburgh: Canongate Books, 2007.

Schulman, Kori. "The Digital Transition: How the Presidential Transition Works in the Social Media Age." October 31, 2016. *The White House—President Barack Obama.* ObamaWhiteHouse.archives.gov/blog/2016/10/31/digital-transition-how-presidential-transition-works-social-media-age.

Swarns, Rachel L. "First Chores? You Bet." *New York Times.* February 21, 2009. NYTimes.com/2009/02/22/fashion/22firstp.html.

The White House. "Barack Obama." 2020. WhiteHouse.gov/about-the-white-house/presidents/barack-obama.

# Acknowledgments

I remember exactly where I was when Barack Obama got elected the first time. I remember the joy and jubilation I felt as a black woman to witness the inauguration of the first black president. I want to thank and acknowledge Barack Obama for being such an inspiration. I am honored to share his story with young people.

Thank you to the team at Callisto and my editor, Kristen Depken, for your patience with me! Thank you to my family for always supporting me! And thank you to the children who read this book. I hope you find inspiration here, too! —T. L.

# About the Author

**TONYA LESLIE, PhD,** is an educator, keynote speaker, and researcher. She studies issues related to educational equity and literacy. She is also a writer. Her other children's books include *So Other People Would Be Also Free: The Real Story of Rosa Parks for Kids.* Tonya splits her time between New York City and Belize, Central America. She enjoys visiting museums, swimming, and reading on airplanes. Learn more about her work at TonyaLeslie.com.